Praise for Exit, pursued by a bear

What an inspired collection! The lines between reality and the stage, between life and art, between past and present—they're all blurred into an exciting whirligig of poetry based on Shakespeare's stage directions. You don't have to be a Shakespeare nut to fall in love with this collection, but these poems are sure to cast a spell that won't be easily broken by man or beast . . . a wonderful piece of literature that should be studied along with Shakespeare's plays in English classes around the world.

>—Robert Lee Brewer, author *Solving the World's Problems* and editor of *Poet's Market*

As a poet, Joseph Mills keeps a close eye on the ordinary, knowing that, at any moment, the extraordinary is bound to flash forth. And it's that flashing forth that most people miss. Yet when they read about it in deceptively easy-to-understand terms, they immediately recognize a truth, a truth that they missed. But now that they have been awakened to the possibility of spotting it for themselves, they can go out there into their lives and look for it themselves.

>—John P. O'Grady, author *Grave Goods* and *Pilgrims to the Wild*

Praise for other books by Joseph Mills

Disturbingly brilliant, breaking boundaries with shocking immediacy, *This Miraculous Turning* lays bare a trail of poems that navigate extreme terrain. These poems sear, disfigure, dismantle and reconstruct the truths of a history that informs otherness and taboos. Joseph Mills offers lyrical beauty inside a turbulent storm of history, memory, and hope that dances the bones of the nameless child free and gives flesh to the spirits in an explicit celebration of love and grace.

>—Jaki Shelton Green, author of *Breath of a Song: New and Selected Poems*

I have been reading Joseph Mills' work for years, but this, his fourth collection, is my favorite. In *Sending Christmas Cards to Huck & Hamlet*, Mills examines a lifetime of reading—from Westerns to fairy tales, poetry to Hamlet—looking for the other story, the darker story, the story that changes as one moves from being child to parent, student to teacher, youth to adult. Ultimately, Mills' poems do what poetry should do: simplify the complicated and complicate the seemingly simple. You'll never think of Rapunzel as a victim again.

— Lori Ostlund, author of *After the Parade: A Novel*

Joseph Mills is a poet who understands that Love's great nemesis isn't Hate but Time. Time and again, the poems in *Love and Other Collisions* explore the inherent pain created when Love and Time meet. This book stands as a chronicle of the speaker's growth from a hopeful youth to a father carving out the best life he can for his own children to a man who is a helpless witness to his mother's battle with Alzheimer's disease. In the words of one poem, Mills "show[s] how you [can] make something of your life if only you [can] stand enough punishment over the years." *Love and Other Collisions* is at once ambitious, unflinching, and tender—It is definitely a must-read.

— Shaindel Beers, author of *A Brief History of Time*

To Joe Mills a glass of wine reveals a little of "the almost infinite risk in being who we are." *Angels, Thieves, and Winemakers* is, then, a collection of revelations, truths to be found in and about wine. Witty, mordant, melancholy, funny—these bright poems fix and illumine the many moods we may encounter in a bottle of happy red. I shall recommend this volume most heartedly, saying, "Here, I think this / will help make things a little better."

— Fred Chappell, author of *Dance of Shadows*, and former Poet Laureate of North Carolina

Exit, pursued by a bear

Also by Joseph Mills

POETRY
Somewhere During the Spin Cycle
Angels, Thieves, and Winemakers
Love and Other Collisions
Sending Christmas Cards to Huck & Hamlet
This Miraculous Turning

NONFICTION
A Guide to North Carolina's Wineries (with Danielle Tarmey)

ACADEMIC CRITICISM
Reading Richard Brautigan's Trout Fishing in America
A Century of the Marx Brothers
Reading Louis L'Amour's Hondo

EXIT, PURSUED BY A BEAR

Poems in both tragical and comedic veins inspired, evoked, prompted, triggered, and summoned by the stage directions in the dramatic works of the esteemed William Shakespeare

Joseph Mills

Press 53
Winston-Salem

Press 53, LLC
PO Box 30314
Winston-Salem, NC 27130

First Edition

Copyright © 2016 by Joseph Mills

All rights reserved, including the right of reproduction in whole or in part in any form. For permission, contact publisher at Editor@Press53.com, or at the address above.

Cover design by Kevin Morgan Watson

Author photo by Diana Greene

Printed on acid-free paper
ISBN 978-1-941209-36-3

For the good teachers, in all your various apparitions

Acknowledgments

Thanks to the following publications where these poems (or earlier versions of them) first appeared.

Blue Lotus Review: "Enter Horatio," "Exit Falstaff"
Catch & Release: "Dead March," "Enter Juliet," "Enter Prince of Wales..." "Enter Shylock," "Exit with the Body"
Cobalt Review: "Enter Lady Macbeth, reading a letter," "Enter Romeo and Juliet, above, at the window"
DASH Journal: "Exit at one door with the body of his father"
Foliate Oak: "Enter Rumor, Painted Full of Tongues"
Foundling Review: "Enter Cassandra, raving"
Germ Magazine: "Enter the King in his nightgown, alone" (as "Enter King"), "Enter the Queen with her hair about her ears," "Enter Ophelia," "Enter Polonius," "Ferdinand and Miranda playing at chess"
Gingerbread House: "Enter Hamlet"
The Indian River Review: "Enter Falstaff wearing a buck's head"
Innisfree Journal: "The clock striketh," "Enter Poet, Painter, Jeweler, Merchant, and Mercer, at several doors" (as "Enter Gardeners"), "She picks up some pieces"
Ishaan Literary Review: "Enter Pericles, Wet," "Exit, the Bastard," "Flourish. Exeunt all but Hamlet"
Lowestoft Chronicle: "Enter the travellers"
Literary Orphans: "Enter at the other end of the churchyard, Friar Laurence, with a lantern, crow, and spade," "Enter *Jacques*, and Lords ([like]) *Foresters*) [with a dead deer]," "Falstaff Riseth Up"
MadHat Lit: "Enter Cinna, The Poet," "Enter the Duchess in a white sheet," "Enter a company of mutinous Citizens..."
Marathon Literary Review: "Enter Hortensio with his head broke," "Enter Steward, with many bills in his hand"
Metazen: "Exit Running. Attendants Follow"
The Minetta Review: "Jupiter descends in thunder and lightning, sitting upon an eagle."
The Misfit Journal: "Enter Lucio and two other gentleman," "Exit"
New Orleans Review: "Exit, pursued by a bear" and "Exit at another door with the body of his son"

One: "Enter Othello and Desdemona in her bed"
Punchnel's: "Enter a Messenger with two heads and a hand," "Enter Richard and Buckingham in rotten armor, marvelous ill-favored"
Raleigh Review: "Enter Ghost"
Tar River Poetry: "Enter Ambassadors of France"
Two Hawks Quarterly: "Enter Duke (disguised)," "Enter Viola, a Captain, and Sailors," "Enter Helena"
Upstart: A Journal of English Renaissance Studies: "Enter Armado," "Enter Bottom," "Enter Friar John," "Enter Kate," "Enter Lady Macbeth," "Enter Time, the Chorus" (as "Off Stage")

And, once again, I am indebted to the MakeGroup of Bob King, Betsy Towns, and Dean Wilcox, the initial audience for many of these poems, and to John O'Grady, who is generous with his critical eye.

Contents

Enter the Duchess in a white sheet	1
Exit at another door with the body of his son	2
Exit at one door with the body of his father	3
Exit with the body	4
Dead March	5
Enter a Messenger with two heads and a hand	6
She picks up some pieces	7
Enter Kate	9
Enter Hortensio with his head broke	10
Enter aloft the drunkard…	11
Enter the Queen with her hair about her ears	12
Enter Richard and Buckingham in rotten armor, marvelous ill-favored	13
The clock striketh	14
Exeunt omnes, as fast as may be, frightened	15
Enter Armado	16
Enter Romeo and Juliet, above, at the window	17
Enter Juliet	18
Enter Friar John	19
Enter at the other end of the churchyard, Friar Laurence, with a lantern, crow, and spade	20
Enter Romeo. Enter Juliet	21
Enter Bottom	22
[Exit, the Bastard]	23
Enter Gardeners	24
Enter the travellers	25
Falstaff Riseth Up	26
Enter Prince of Wales…	27
Enter Falstaff wearing a buck's head	28
Enter Rumor, Painted Full of Tongues	29
Enter the King in his nightgown, alone	30
Enter Shylock	31
Exeunt Portia and Nerissa	33
Enter Benedick, alone	34
Enter Innogen	35

Enter Ambassadors of France	36
Exit Falstaff	37
Enter Cinna, the poet	38
Enter *Jacques*, and *Lords* ([like]) *Foresters*) [with a dead deer]	39
Enter Ghost	40
Flourish. Exeunt all but Hamlet	41
Enter Gertrude	42
Enter Ophelia	43
Enter Hamlet	44
Enter Polonius	45
Enter Horatio	46
Enter Othello and Desdemona in her bed	47
Enter Viola, a Captain, and Sailors	48
Enter Cassandra Raving	49
Enter Helena	50
Enter Poet, Painter, Jeweler, Merchant, and Mercer, at several doors	51
Enter Steward, with many bills in his hand	52
Enter Duke [disguised]	53
Enter Lucio and two other gentlemen	54
Exit Running. Attendants Follow	55
Enter Lady Macbeth, reading a letter	56
Enter Lady Macbeth	57
Thunder and Lightning. Enter Three Witches	58
Oboes and Torches	59
Enter Pericles, wet	60
Enter a company of mutinous Citizens, with staves, clubs, and other weapons	61
Jupiter descends in thunder and lightning, sitting upon an eagle	62
Hermione, like a statue	63
Enter Time, the Chorus	64
Ferdinand and Miranda playing at chess	65
Exit, pursued by a bear	66
Enter King Henry	69
Exit	71
Sources of Stage Directions	73
Author Biography	75

*All the world's a stage
And all the men and women merely players
They have their exits and their entrances...*
                        — Jacques, *As You Like It*

If you read Shakespeare's stage directions, all the gore and violence is right in there.
                        — Teller

Enter the Duchess in a white sheet

Those working wardrobe know
there are two kinds of sheets
in Shakespeare, white and bloody.

The first often becomes the second
and then becomes the first again:
wedding to wounding to winding.

It's a common progression,
perhaps the fundamental one;
still, each time he must start,

as every writer does,
contemplating white sheets,
then staining them, one by one,

until by the end, ink-crammed
with rhymes and bodies,
they sail ever graveward.

Exit at another door with the body of his son

    Some Saturdays, back from London,
    he would take the twins to the park,
    and sit on a bench, amid the wives
    and maids. Sometimes he worked
    on scenes in his head,
                    mostly he didn't.

    He would watch children play
    the way he had,
               the way they always have,
    running and wrestling,
    hair-pulling and pretending
    sticks were swords,
                    stabbing,
    killing one another and being killed,
    again
        and again
              and again.

    Once Hamnet fell from a tree,
    hit the ground and didn't move;
    Judith began an odd keening,
    her face in her hands.
    He had bolted to his prone son,
    knelt and had heard
    giggling.
            How astonishing
    to have death suddenly arrive
    then disappear just as quickly.

Exit at one door with the body of his father

A dead parent is difficult
to move
but it has to be done.

So you clean out
closets and file drawers.
Cancel subscriptions.
Put the house on the market.

Bit by bit,
you drag the body
from the stage
so the story can go on.

Exit with the body

The body gets pulled into the wings
and pushed wherever there's space,
something that gets harder to find
as the run goes along.

The guts lugged away each night,
the lopped off hands and heads,
pile up
        until even the loading dock
and parking lot behind the theater
overflow with limbs
                  and torsos.

Behind the curtain the remains
of these dreams, a landscape
of wounds and wreckage.

Dead March

Why the orderly procession,
the neat rows,
the solemn filing in
                      and out?

Why the polite contemplation
of the black box?

There should be a howling,
a roiling of people
coming and going,
not just stage left and right,
but through windows and walls,
up flats and backdrops
like Harpo in *A Night at the Opera*.

Don't bother turning
to locate an exit;
every direction is one.

Enter a Messenger with two heads and a hand

There's enough work in these plays
to make an okay living,
especially if you can do a few money moves
before the news you have goes public.

The trick is to keep your mouth shut
no matter what you're carrying
or who the recipient
and to not react
no matter what they give you:
coins, curses, blows.

Mostly it's letters and announcements,
but there is the occasional head,
which can be messy
because no one ever bothers
to box them up properly.
These you often can upsell
to include a platter
instead of a bag
(the profit margin's in the surcharges)
because it's not just about delivery,
but display. You're like a waiter,
showcasing a meal,
but it's not about you.
That's the key.
You go on,
deliver the news, or hands,
or whatever, and get off.
Just do that, and you'll be fine.
You'll make enough
to feed the family,
save a little for retirement,
and you'll be alive at the end.

She picks up some pieces

Each day she was free
to have anything she wanted
to eat or drink.

Nothing was denied her
                     at the table
        even if she requested:

*A small half goat-milk no foam latte
        and half snake-milk cocoa-less mocha
                in a pre-warmed silk venti cup.*

But she knew it was an illusion
        of choice   of control.

No matter how large,
                the castle
was still a box and she
        a prize within.

Each day someone asked
what she wanted
        and what she wanted

was a sunburst telecaster
with humbucker pickups

what she wanted was
opponents
                who would play hard

what she wanted was
a solo one way ticket,
a storyline that didn't end
in marriage
            or suicide,

    the keys to the cars
                            and doors

    and these could be hers

    but what she wanted
              was to not be asked
                         and not be given.

Enter Kate

Before the banquet had even ended, someone had uploaded her speech from an iphone, and it was being forwarded and posted and linked. An agent emailed her that night, offering a contract and laying out a familiar trajectory. First, the biography, full of details, like tying up her sister and striking the servants, but with, of course, the redemption narrative—bad girl grows up (that Prince Hal thing but with a gender twist). Perfect for daytime TV and the talking heads circuit. Then a few self-help and childrens' books. Eventually a show and brand of her own—*Kate!*—complete with clothing, makeup, perfume, all the products of fem-glam capitalism.

But it was Petruchio who responded, claiming to already be in talks with William Morris and CAA. He was her manager with dreams of being Colonel Parker (if the Colonel had thought of himself as more important and talented than Elvis). So the agent went to work on him, telling tales of possible roles and packaging: reality series, award show hosting, movie franchises. It was annoying because Petruchio, hell, he was just biceps and a jaw—virile not viral—but it was necessary because Kate, that girl, she could be something special if she was handled right.

Enter Hortensio with his head broke.

Sometimes Kate hits him hard enough
lights flash in his eyes, he gets nauseous,
and he can't find his way backstage.
It's a familiar feeling. There was the time
at school the PE teacher had insisted
they learn rugby, and he and Timmy
had banged heads as they both ran
away from the ball. There was the time
at the pool, Bobby had tripped him,
and he had skull-smacked a railing
then slapsticked backwards into the water.
There was the time, late for a meeting,
he head-butted the conference door
that Susan had locked behind her.
At least now, it's a choice. Kind of.
Although he hopes he won't end up
slurring and stumbling, damaged
like an old boxer or football player,
like them, he needs to earn a living,
so, like them, he agrees to be beaten
for the amusement of those watching.

Enter aloft the drunkard ...

Her father came into the auditorium.

Her father came into the auditorium and waved.

Her father came into the auditorium and waved to her then stumbled on the steps.

Her father came into the auditorium and waved to her then stumbled on the steps, and several rows away her mother looked at a phone and pretended not to notice, sure that people were glancing back and forth and whispering their names and words like "drinking" and "divorce."

Her father came into the auditorium and waved to her then did as he had done so often in so many places, and although he may have simply lost his balance, no one else had trouble just getting to a seat, no one else had such difficulty performing the simplest acts of parenting, and she knew he had come just to make a point, to play the public role of Dad, and she was supposed to be grateful, but she didn't feel gratitude, she felt dizzy and nauseous, as if she was about to fall, and she felt herself looking elsewhere as if she didn't notice the man sprawled on the steps, and she felt the watching and whispering, and she felt the familiar sense of her skin hardening on her face, like a mask, and then she turned its fixed smile towards the vague shapes arrayed before her, the figures that resembled people, but none that she knew.

Enter the Queen with her hair about her ears.

In second grade, she cut her hair,
taking the blunt art class scissors
and squeezing off a thick lock
in the middle of her forehead.

Her mother had grounded her,
saying, "We have to look at you,"
making it clear her body
was not hers
to do with as she chose,
but a display for others.

In high school, she shaved her head
explaining it cleared her vision.
We were impressed by her refusal
to play the role,
                but we also understood
that gesture too was a performance;
                      hair and clothes
were ads
        warnings
                      bulletins
conveying information
about danger
    about wantonness
        about desire
about who had begun
to become undone.

Enter Richard and Buckingham in rotten armor, marvelous ill-favored.

You went forward confident, feeling good
about your prospects, but afterwards,
seeing photographs and video clips,
you realize how marvelous ill favored
you were, especially compared to the others,
the ones in the expensive wardrobes,
the ones with the extensive walk-in closets.
You were defeated as soon as you got dressed.
Those watching knew it; everyone did, but you.

The clock striketh

If exiting you feel the same
as when you entered,

go to the box office
and demand a refund,

run backstage
to where the actors are
removing makeup,
and stand in the doorway,
an accusatory ghost,

keep the ticket stub,
so you can explain
your account is unbalanced,
you're owed those hours

because that's the contract—
part of your life in return
for being changed
                somehow—

and maybe Death will listen,
after all he too was there,
as he is at every performance,
in the back, taking notes,
attentive,
                hopeful.

Exeunt omnes, as fast as may be, frightened

Afterwards, at the bar,
some will admit, *Jesus,*
I couldn't get out of there
fast enough. They may
even display bruises
or rips in their clothes
as a type of testament.

And some won't speak of it
the animal bolting,
              the abandoning
everyone   everything
the wanting only to get away
as fast as may be.

And some will make it a story
or joke, a Keystone Kops moment,
trying to transform it
into slapstick and pratfalls,
to shape the fear
        into something else
                  something
that makes it
        possible to bear.

Enter Armado

It was painful now to remember
how gratified he'd been at being named
Ambassador to Navarre, the stationary
and business cards he'd had made,
the conviction it was the start of his career.
Then, over the years, the realization
his name never made the shortlists
that circulated when openings came up.
Worse was hearing about his peers
getting positions in dramas by Calderon
and Lope de Vega and all the talk
of "The Golden Age of Spanish Theatre"
while he was stuck in a backwater acting
the buffoon for puerile young royalty.
Some nights, he was tempted to head
to the airport instead of the theater,
but he prided himself on his professionalism
(plus there was the house his wife loved
and the kids in school), so he kept bowing
and fulfilling his duties as clownish foil,
even as he fantasized about a re-assignment
to the Danish court, or Venice, or, hell,
even Scotland, some place the job mattered
and the royalty were important enough
to have their names on the title page.

Enter Romeo and Juliet, above, at the window

Because it all happened so quickly,
she never had a chance to ask him,
some of the embarrassing questions,
like about Rosaline. Why was he with her?
How far had it gone? Or, what he intended
to do for a living? Or what exactly he did
hanging around with his friends all day?

Those would have come later. With the doubts.
The regrets. The accusations and recriminations.
The nights wondering where he was. The parties
having to watch him eye other young girls.
The tragedy would have been the questions
that couldn't be stabbed or poisoned or fled,
the ones they would have had to live with.

Enter Juliet

      Later she would have regretted the naked photos
      and lascivious tweets. She would have looked
      through yearbook pictures and shook her head
      at the hair and clothing and posing, at the sequins,
      at how oblivious she was to her own gawkiness,
      at how she had thought she knew everything
      of importance. Later…
                                    but there is no later for her.
      No stepping from a shower in front of a mirror
      and thinking, *My God, what happened to my ass?*
      No dressertop of expensive creams for her hands.
      No nights sprawled on the couch with someone
      who, despite her weight and wrinkles and gray,
      feels for her in a way that beggars description.
      No waking, stiff, together, morning after morning.

Enter Friar John

Certainly he had a good excuse
for not taking the letter to Romeo;
an ill colleague who needed him
was a better use of his time and talents
than being a delivery boy
for a couple of horny teens.

Or maybe he was leery of Friar Laurence
whose tendency to meddle
and make things unduly complicated
had resulted in a fat file of complaints
from annoyed parents and parishioners.

But probably there was no sick friar,
and he had just been drinking
with other messengers in a pub,
telling tales of how thankless
their jobs were, how payment
was often curses or blows
with people only knowing your name
when you screwed up.
They had kept on ordering
just one more round,
                              just one more,
letting the story go on without them,
believing they could join it later,
and that tomorrow, or even next week,
would be soon enough to deliver
the catalogues, Amazon boxes,
death warrants, whatever it was
in the bags on the floor at their feet.

Enter at the other end of the churchyard, Friar Laurence, with a lantern, crow, and spade

Look, all I'm asking is Why the spade?
After all, he knows she's in a tomb,
he helped put her in it.
So, maybe it's just a cheap symbol
for the audience—"Grave Work!"—
or maybe he simply scooped up
what he could hold. But maybe,
maybe, in his haste, he has slipped
into old patterns, taking tools
he's used before. Some say
they've seen lights in the cemetery
at night, that someone's been
rooting up bones and bodies
like plants. Or does he suspect
he'll find something he'll need
to bury? I don't know, but
if the tools make the man,
we should dig a little deeper
because something's suspicious
about this meddling monk. Maybe
he doesn't know what he's doing,
but maybe, maybe, we don't.

Enter Romeo. Enter Juliet.

The fifth grade performs *Romeo and Juliet* each May,
and the whole school attends, so the students see
this boy-girl tale, this double suicide, in kindergarten
then again and again and again and again and again.
No one expects a play about Elmo or Dora the Explorer,
(although at least she's a strong girl with the sense
not to get overwrought about a muppet). But it is odd,
this annual insistence on a world of such violence.
Perhaps the problem is the season. This isn't a tale
to tell in spring—it is no love story—but rather one
for October. Acknowledge the play as the nightmare
it is, how it casts our children as Juliets and Romeos,
how it forces us to watch as they kill themselves
vainly, and then how we are expected to applaud.

Enter Bottom

Drinking Budweiser on the hood
of Gary's Oldsmobile Cutlass,
we looked at the lights on the lake
and talked about what we might do—
ask out Cathy or Cindy or Nancy;
become lawyers, doctors,
hell, maybe even President;
tell off that son-of-a-bitch
of an assistant manager,
of a teacher, of a coach—

and, right then, we believed
we could. We could
leave the town, somehow,
and be transformed.
We had heard stories
that it had happened,
tales of someone's sibling
going away and becoming
the type of person
you saw in magazines.

As the night went on,
we would get louder,
not knowing or caring
if anyone heard us,
our voices a melody
of yearning and desperation
splintering against the trees.

We just wanted something
to do, some kind of role,
any of them, all of them,
ones that meant something
if only to asses like us.

[Exit, the Bastard]

Ellen texted him to check out that week's *Shout*, so he went to the deli by his office and leafed through a copy during lunch. In an interview towards the back, John was promoting his latest group—Pulled Pork. The photo showed that he had added a bandana to his glower, probably to hide the hairline. It was all the usual posturing until John started slagging his earlier bands and claimed that theirs had broken up over a comma, an argument about whether the merch should read *Exit the Bastard* or *Exit, the Bastard*. The pull quote read: "It's good to be playing with legit musicians, and not a bunch of fucking grammarians." He didn't remember any argument or any merch for that matter. In fact, it was John who had been the English major and who had come up with that name and the other ones—The Jack Cades, The Lawyer Killers, Titus and Ronicus, The Bastards—trying out variations in his notebook. The rest of them hadn't cared, and they had ignored his strutting around and his constant twaddle. Now, he was rewriting history, acting like he hadn't authored any of it, acting like he didn't have a fucking college degree.

And yet, in a way, John was right; he hadn't belonged. He knew it the fifth or sixth show when a beer bottle got thrown into the audience and hit a kid in the face. "Got thrown." That's how he had described it once to Ellen. But it had been him. Trying out a gesture. One that had provoked a few drunks to charge the stage. John had gleefully kicked them backwards, howling. A crazed king at the parapet's edge, one who would never be happier.

That night, even though they had several shows booked, he had walked out, not bothering to say a word to anyone, just like a real bastard, closing the backstage door as quietly as a parenthesis.

Enter Gardeners

At the farmer's market, we're charmed
by the floppy hats, and welly boots,
the bouquets of flowers and baskets of fruit,

and although gardeners believe
in the need for blades
                                and black seasons
in prunings
               and uprootings
in soil made rich by the rotting
of cabbages and kings,

they smile as they offer samples
of peaches, slices of tomatoes,
cuttings of lavender, the bounty
of this seductive green world,
that tongues forth from our graves.

Enter the Travellers

Twice Shakespeare disappeared.
The "lost years" they're called
by scholars although he knew
where he was. Maybe it was surfing
in Costa Rica or climbing in Tibet,
but more likely he sailed
into Boston or Savannah,
then started hitchhiking West.
He talked and drank and smoke
with whomever he met.
Lewis and Clark. Kerouac.
Custer. Crazy Horse.
He hung out for a while
with other ex-pats in Hollywood
then headed North to the Bay Area
where he sat in with The Warlocks,
Jerry teaching him bar chords
in exchange for hearing madrigals.
Dylan mentions it in *Blonde on Blonde*,
but that's not good enough
for academics. They want to find
buried somewhere in an archive
a receipt for the pink Cadillac he rented
to drive Route 66. The initials WS
scratched in places on a waiver.
But they won't. In those years,
wherever he was,
he was just trucking,
keeping a low profile,
and not writing a thing,
not even a postcard to Anne.

Falstaff Riseth Up

Posters in classrooms and bars
listed synonyms for drinking:
fap, cashiered, spongy, rouse,

or terms for sex: *making the beast with two backs,*

or insults: *you starveling, you elf-skin,*
you dried neat's tongue, you bull's pizzle.
You filthy bung. You basket-hilt stale juggler.
You scullion! You rampallian! You fustilarian!
Thou cream faced loon. Thou leathern-jerkin,
   crystal-button, knot-pated, agatering,
   puke-stocking, caddis-garter,
   smooth tongue Spanish pouch.

At first, we read them with delight
then with a vague sense of diminishment.
We too drank and fucked and swore,
but with nothing like such . . . such . . .
with nothing like . . .
   . . . goddamnit. . .
      god . . . damnit. . .

Resentfully we mouthed our meager words,
the shreds and patches of our mother tongue.

Enter Prince of Wales...

Doing bong hits between classes,
under the bleachers
or behind the dumpsters,
we knew we were disappointments
to our parents who wanted us to be
the kids who got good grades,
talked of college,
had obvious ambitions,
and we honestly thought we could be
if we chose to,
and even that we would be,
eventually.
We would.
This dissolution,
this dissipation,
was only temporary.
In a couple years, we would throw off
our loose behavior,
rise and shine,
put our shoulders to some wheel,
etc.
                etc.
                                etc.
O, everyone would be astonished
as we became who we were
destined to become,
but that would be later
after these salad days
when we had a muse of fire
cradled in our hands,
showing us the world
was an insubstantial pageant,
a dumb show whose parts
we were refusing to play
at least just yet.

Enter Falstaff wearing a buck's head

Within minutes of his arrival,
photos were posted on Facebook,
and he twittered a few selfies
at #illfeelwretchedtomorrow.
By the weekend, he had become
an Internet meme—Fatman Sez—
jumping out of Halloween caskets
or leering from famous pictures
and commenting on everything
from health care to holiday sales.

Who could resist posting the image
of a lascivious drunk in costume,
one humiliated for our amusement?

Later, we'll try to scrub our accounts
and issue denials. We'll pretend
that wasn't us, nearby, wearing
some animal head of our own.
We'll claim youth and ignorance,
insist that it was a one-time thing.

Later we'll realize most of our friends,
perhaps even most of our lives,
should have been in quotation marks.

Enter Rumor, Painted Full of Tongues

My daughter tells me Miley Cyrus is pregnant,
but she and her friends can't agree if the father
is Jay-Z or Eminem. It might not matter anyway
because Sarah thinks she'll get a divortion.
I explain that it's pronounced abortion,
and she asks how it's done. Is it just a shot?
Because that's what Trish has said. Her cousin
has a friend who got one after she got pregnant.
She got a shot and the baby just went away.
But, my daughter says, she's also heard
you can get a shot if you want to get pregnant.
That's what Grace's step-mom did. She got shot
in the leg, but you also can get shot in the butt,
and, you can even get two or three shots
if you want to have twins or triplets,
and there doesn't even need to be a father
although she thinks Grace does have a dad
because she's never heard anyone say she doesn't
and that's the kind of thing people talk about,
but what's kind of scary, my daughter says,
is that she knows drugs also mess a baby up,
not in a two-headed way or anything,
but in a born with six fingers, not normal, way,
and Miley Cyrus definitely does drugs,
more than Selena Gomez or Justin Bieber
who have been in rehab together, maybe
that's even where they met. No one knows
if it's a boy or girl or if it has a name yet,
but, she tells me, we should find out soon
maybe tomorrow; it will be on Instagram
or the news and people will tell her at school
and she'll let me know as soon as they do.

Enter the King in his nightgown, alone

She doesn't know why he seems familiar
until he launches into a soliloquy,
and she recognizes something in his voice.
He works at Modern Ford across town,
and last year he had tried to sell her
a used Taurus. She had been interested,
but he had pushed so hard she had left
and had ended up buying a Jeep instead.
When she had walked away, he had acted
betrayed, as if simply coming had meant
commitment, but that's not how it works,
there or here. She had been willing to listen,
but she'll probably slip out at intermission
because she's not buying it this time either.

Enter Shylock

The title so annoys him
he doesn't say it out loud.
Instead he talks about "the show"
and hopes no one notices.
Because it's his play. Google his name,
then any of the other characters.
People wait for his entrance.
They've come to see him
although, to be fair,
the woman has some good lines
and that bit with the boxes.

So, if not *Shylock*, call it
Shylock and Portia. After all,
they own the courtroom scene.
They dominate the posters.
They get the marquee billing.
Who gives a damn about
what's his name. Antonio.
A nobody
        and the playwright knew it.
At best, the title's puzzling;
at worst a failure of nerve,
a lack of imagination,
or just the act of a prick
who won't give credit
where it's due.

But he knows it's blasphemy
to criticize
        The Bard.
He might as well spit on a Bible,
so he bites his tongue and mouths
his appreciation of the part.
Laughing or crying

isn't going to change the fact
he's not the merchant,
but the merchandise
to be cut up each night and fed
to a ravenous, merciless, audience.

Exeunt Portia and Nerissa

Your period starts the first day of vacation
        of your honeymoon
                of your new job.

You go into the woods
        and come back with a baby
                or empty handed.

The banditti rob you
        ignore you
                make you their leader.

The coffee spills.
        The car breaks down.
                The doctor explains the results.

Afterwards you may try to measure
        what's deserved, or not
                why what happened happened

but first there is the broken glass
        the blood-stained clothes
                the calls to make.

Enter Benedick, alone

the pleasure is in watching

                                      him

eavesdropping his way
towards marriage

                                      and her

manipulated against
the current of her own words

                                      and

the crumpling of convictions,
the surrendering to joy,

then the dizzying turn,
her insistence he kill

                                      Claudio

his rapid spin
from refusal to willingness,

love harnessed in a breath
to violence and vengeance

love quicksilver

                                      and nothing
                                      if not disorienting.

Enter Innogen

She enters but has no lines,
a ghost character, and like her,
your name is in stories
in which you have no part.

It's written in books
strangers have on their shelves.
It's doodled on pages
stored in closets and filing cabinets.

It appears in letters of people
you don't know,
and on lists for invitations
you've never received.

Someone travelling a highway
is suddenly saying your name.

Enter Ambassadors of France

When he arrived in London,
he cobbled together work
as a freelancer, placing pieces
about bear-baiting and bowling,
quail-fighting and quoits.
A lyric about a duchess
playing shrove-groat
gained some notice,
but it was his reporting
on tennis that served
as his entry into court.
Some royals recognized
the value of poetic PR
and used him to spin
stories of their prowess,
which he did willingly.
Later, he would insist
you could tell how someone
would wield a scepter
by how they held a racquet.
After he retired to Stratford,
spending his time golfing
and managing his portfolio,
sometimes people would ask
if he missed the city's pomp
and privilege. He didn't.
What he missed was watching
a match's back-and-forth,
drinking ale, eating hazelnuts,
and feeling at each point
he was seeing more clearly
the players, the game,
and how it could be played.

Exit Falstaff

Falstaff thought the shout-out at the end
of *The Second Part of Henry the Fourth*
meant job security, so he bought a new car,
booked a cruise, put a deposit on a beach house,
but the story went differently, as it often does.
He died. Off-stage. We make our plans,
and then the phone rings. Or doesn't.
The doctor just wants to know the symptoms;
it doesn't matter if the tickets are non-refundable.

Enter Cinna, the poet

He has the misfortune to have the wrong name
in the wrong place at the wrong time. He is not
Cinna, the conspirator, but Cinna, the poet.
It doesn't matter. A mob will do what mobs do,
finding any justification for the violence it desires.
"Tear him for his bad verses," someone shouts.
"Tear him for his bad verses," another agrees,
and we laugh darkly, even us poets, especially
us poets. We are not Caesars, rulers, or soldiers,
but we'll be torn down and torn up just the same.
The names and nouns don't matter. The verbs,
the verbs, determine all. And don't place hope
in the adjective. There are no good verses.
At least none good enough to save you.

Enter *Jacques,* and *Lords* ([like]) *Foresters*) [with a dead deer]

                      So much
has been chopped up and off
in these plays,
        so much
has been lost
        the editors strain
to make them coherent,
splinting and bandaging
with parentheses and parentheses
within parentheses, italics, commas,
periods, capitalization,
trying to suture closed
the ruptures.

But the prince, as he dies,
points to the void
that can't be glossed
by words or grammar.

Iago says, "What you know,
        you know."

And Lavinia,
        Lavinia says nothing.
She doesn't even move her stumps.

Enter Ghost

He knew about ghosts

how sometimes they appear
to everyone, and sometimes
only you can see them,

how you listen
because you think
since they're dead
and know the great secret now
they must know
other things as well,

how they are wounds
wearing human faces.

Flourish. Exeunt all but Hamlet.

They took him to Wittenberg
and helped unpack the van.
His dad bought a case of beer
for the mini-fridge;
his mother made sure
the sheets fit the bed.
They met his dormmates,
who seemed nice enough
although hard to tell apart.
They gave him more advice,
then, finally, said goodbye.

He found it odd to be
on his own and not feeling
constantly watched. No one
thought they knew him
or saw him as Junior.
They asked things like
if he had picked a major,
the college equivalent of
What do you want to be
when you grow up?
As if you could decide to be
something simply by choosing.
It was exhilarating,
the sense of possibilities
the first weeks on campus,
the feeling he could be
a lawyer or doctor or professor.
He could even end up being
someone whose portrait
would hang in the commons
for something he had done,
someone whose achievements
people would study in books
for years to come.

Enter Gertrude

His self-absorption infuriated her.
He didn't seem to know or care
if people were waiting, always acting
as if he had no responsibilities.
While she packed for trips,
he would be off god-knows-where
doing god-knows-what, and
when he would finally turn up,
he would say something like
all he needed could be put in a nutshell.
What this ended up meaning was, No
he hadn't picked out his clothes yet.

He never saw his own hypocrisy,
how if "the readiness was all,"
then, damnit, why was he never ready?
Why were they always waiting
in the car, or at the dinner table,
for him to finally shamble up,
unfocused and untucked?
When they took him to the dorm
and she said goodbye,
she didn't feel sweet sorrow,
but liberation. At last, she thought
as she walked away. At last.

Enter Ophelia

She fills notebooks with lists:

of presents she might send him
while he's at Wittenberg,
of who would be invited
to the wedding if it was big
or if it was small, of menus,
of honeymoon destinations,
of baby names, of flowers
she might like in the garden,
of what she would need to take
for a trip to England or Italy,
of what she would need to pack
for an elopement
or if she ran away herself
or if her father finally agreed
to let her go to college.
One notebook outfits dorm rooms,
singles, doubles, triples, quads,
another has various changes
she would make to the castle,
and another has possible names
if she ever had a small B&B.

Each day, she writes a new one,
imagining possible futures,
reassuring herself she has one.

Enter Hamlet

She gives the remembrances back.
The letters. The birthday cards.
His dress shirt she wore in bed.
The stuffed animal from the fair.
The mix-tapes. The bracelets.
She boxes them all, an act of strength,
since she's the one being jilted,

and he can't bear to look at them,
these objects that bear witness.
He wants to walk away. Deny
he gave her aught. But here it is—
scarf, earrings, ticket stubs,
postcards, photo booth strips—
a world of too too solid things.

Enter Polonius

How tiring it was for the women,
to be constantly talked at,
corrected, given unasked for advice.
Even the queen was lectured to,
told what to do, eavesdropped on.
Although she could never admit it,
a part of her must have been relieved,
when her son stabbed him. Finally,
silence, or there would be once
the men finished killing each other.

Enter Horatio

Even at the end, he calls the prince sweet
despite the evidence to the contrary,
the court of corpses, the final body count.

And now, what will he do? Advise Fortinbras
like a next generation Polonius? Return...
where? Where is he from? Who is he?

The enigma isn't Hamlet, but his friend,
the only one who doesn't seem enmeshed
in the court's intrigues, and yet threads

through the action from first scene to last.
Even during the soliloquies, he's there,
listening, in plain sight, and so forgotten.

If they're smart, the Elsinore police
will bring him in for questioning. Something's
suspicious about such self-effacement.

Even his offer to kill himself seems
a gesture, like bringing flowers or a meal
to a sick relative. Still, you have to admire

someone who lives there and survives,
and, if you wonder how he did it, consider
how rarely the question ever comes up.

Enter Othello and Desdemona in her bed

As his hands encircle her throat,
she wants to fight back,
but her training enables her
to stay passive because
this is how the story goes,
and then, in the audience,
a phone plays *Star Wars*,
and the moment is broken,
just the thought of Darth Vader
turning tragedy to camp.

It's funny
how easily Desdemona can be saved

and painful
because we tell our daughters
Call us as they leave the house,
but she too had a phone, there,
within reach, on the nightstand,
so what we should say is...

No...

There is nothing we can say
if they decide to give themselves
over to a tale and its teller,
and there is little we can do
once they've left, except hope
for a random act, a ring tone,
the forgetfulness of strangers,
something to disrupt the story.

Enter Viola, a Captain, and Sailors

Shipwrecked and washed ashore,
disoriented in a strange new world,
it's a story familiar from *The Odyssey,*
Robinson Crusoe, Lost, video games,
our immigrant grandparents,
our divorced parents,
                                         and it will happen
to us as well. The key is to recognize
when you're free from family, you're free
to make yourself into what you can
with what you can. Names, sex, roles,
all can be changed, all but the clock.
When the curtain rises, you must act,
no matter where you find yourself,
no matter what the storm has done.

Enter Cassandra Raving

It's not that we don't believe her,
but that we already know
what she'll say. After all,
unless they're getting paid,
no one who looks to the future
ever sees much good.

The skill would be to foretell,
not the fault in our stars,
not the inevitable bloodslide,
but those moments of joy,
the uncontrollable laughter
with your lover in bed,
the sense of exhilaration
in the grocery store aisle.

This, this is why Cassandra raves,
infuriated by our nodding,
our distracted agreement.
Yes, yes, danger and death
are coming. We know.
We knew as soon as we awoke.

Enter Helena

      She thought the role rubbish
      but she had agreed to it
      because he swore
      there'd be a good part
      in his next play:
                    It Is What It Is,

      something more than the usual
      witch, wench, lady in waiting,
      something, he had hinted,
      with weapons
             and the chance to use them.

      She wasn't naïve.
      She knew the promises of men,
      even ones made in daylight,
      were as slippery as fish.

      But you did what you could
      with what you were given
      and even if all didn't end well,
      and it usually didn't, so be it.
      The trick was to keep acting
                  like it would.

Enter Poet, Painter, Jeweler, Merchant, and Mercer, at several doors

When Anne finally saw some of her husband's plays,
she recognized phrases from discussions they'd had
and exchanges she'd recounted with the jeweler,
dyer, glovemaker, fishmonger ... She didn't mind,
but it was odd to realize all the times she thought
he wasn't listening that he had always been listening,
collecting bits of conversation like change
in a desktop jar, then spending it later in London.
She wondered, after he had returned to Stratford
and stopped writing, how he felt about the words
around him. Did he still deposit them somewhere?
Or, having become a rich gentleman in a New Place,
did he consider them mere farthings and halfpennies,
currency too small to pay much mind to any more.

Enter Steward, with many bills in his hand

When we were young and the landlord knocked,
we would hide in a backroom, giggling,
as if it was a game and our distressed straits
only temporary.

Then, we began opening the door and insisting
we'd have the money soon, and even believing it,
because surely this wasn't how our lives
would always be.

Sometimes we would claim that we'd be happy
to go off and live in the woods. Drink water
and eat roots. Throw what money we had away.
But we wouldn't. Not really.

Now we huddle inside, transfixed by sad stories
of the death of kings, by happy endings and
bloody ones, inured to the implacable bills
silting shut the door.

Enter Duke [disguised]

We see through the disguise,
as we're meant to. Just as we know
who is Rosalind and Viola and Portia
no matter their clothes. We smile
when King Henry, camouflaged
by a cloak, says to his soldiers,
"The king is but a man as I am."
We recognize the deceptions
of Iago and Aaron and Macbeth.
Thus these plays flatter us, and, thus,
fuck us. They make us confident
that we recognize people despite
the changes in wardrobe and hair
and roles over the years, and then
we come home early, get a call
from the police, visit the hospital,
or read an obituary, and realize
we have been the more deceived.
We have had no understanding
of who we have been talking to,
or what stories we've been a part of.
Even as the house lights come up,
when all should have been revealed,
we pore over the program notes,
baffled by what happened and why.

Enter Lucio and two other gentlemen

Others are everywhere
                               in these plays.

Enter the King, Prince of Wales, and others.
Enter the Prince, Poins, with others.
Enter ... with other attendants ... other nobles ...
other citizens ... other soldiers ... other servants ...

Others do their jobs, swell the scenes,
and then go home to their families.

When they were young, others,
like most children, spent hours
learning the letters of their names,
blocking out their names in print,
crayoning their names across sheets
of colored construction paper,
swooping their names in cursive,
filling lined pages of notebooks
with variations of their names,

each instance, a statement—
I am. I am. I am. I am. I am.

Exit Running. Attendants Follow

The crown starts the fight
as it often does, this time because
he sets it in the middle of the family,
assuming they are harmless,
daughters and women, unarmed,
lacking in desire, perhaps
because having held it for so long
he's forgotten what it is to want it.

Then comes the running
for weapons, until even Cordelia
comes back with an army.

It's an old story. Warfare erupting
from the dining room table. It's why
some parents obsessively check the weather,
the stock market, the cupboards,
afraid one day they'll end up outside,
bare-headed, storm-stripped,
and it's why some hesitate to look closely
into the eyes of their children,
because a baby in a cradle
is like a bullet being chambered.

Later smoke will rise from the battlefield
and its blood-birthed centerpiece,
a ring of gold and flowers and thorns,

but the story begins simply.
Here, I say to my father at the door,
stepping in front of my brother,
Let me take that from you.

Enter Lady Macbeth, reading a letter

The husband writes about what happened
on the trip and what was suggested,
and the wife understands why.
It's to have her prod him on;
otherwise, he would have kept silent.
The play understands the machinery

of marriage, about what we do,
not for power, but for our partners,
how time's forge fuses our ambitions,
making us alloys, but also how
it can harden us to a point where,
suddenly,
                      we crack and shear.

Enter Lady Macbeth

She says she's given suck,
so why do they not talk
of the children. Not a word
about how the kids are doing
in college or at new jobs.
No mention of how they'll react
to hearing about their father's successes
or how amused they'll be imagining
the King's retinue in their bedrooms,
splayed among the football trophies,
stuffed animals, and boy band posters.

And yet it may explain the killings
that come and the father's outrage
thinking another's sons will inherit;
he may be looking out for his own
like the Texas mother who put a hit
on her daughter's cheerleading rival.

There is nothing we wouldn't do
for family, we murmur, as we kiss
our children's fontanels,
and swaddle them tightly
in handmade blankets of blood.

Thunder and Lightning. Enter Three Witches

Whenever we manage to get together,
we spend most of the time talking
about the weather and the last time
we got together and the times before that.
We tell the same old stories about family,
friends, colleagues, lovers, about pranks
like the one with those two Scottish guys,
each tale an incantation binding us together.

Oboes and Torches.

He had also wanted trumpets,
cornetts, sacbuts, flutes, and fifes,
at least a dozen instruments
weaving a tapestry of sound,
but all the good horn players
were committed to a gig
at Whitehall, so he had to go
with a couple oboists
and the cheap trick of fire,
barely competent performers
and a primal gimmick,

and it worked. It always did.
Put a flame on stage,
a candle, a taper, a torch,
and the audience would respond
like Pavlovian dogs.

It was effective, it was cheap,
and it was nothing,
                      nothing
like what was in his head.

Enter Pericles, wet

They mist him in the wings
right before he goes on,
and he complains if it's cold,
so they keep it tepid
with a baby bottle warmer
and mix in a little oil,
so he stays wet-looking
throughout the scene.
But just a little. Too much,
and it looks like sweat
rather than water. Too much
and wardrobe complains
the stains won't come out.
Too much and the director
storms, *Goddamnit!*
Quit basting him like a turkey;
spray him like a goddamn plant!
It's ridiculous, they know,
for someone supposedly
wave-thrown,

                              sea-spat.

What they want to do
is fire-hose him or
water-board him
then shove him out,
but instead they mist
and murmur in his ear
right before his cue,
Water dissolves all equally.
No one here knows your name.
You're only in remission.

Enter a company of mutinous Citizens, with staves, clubs, and other weapons.

>Their attention shifts quickly
>from politics to poetry:
>*Tear him for his bad verses!*
>*Tear him for his bad verses!*
>A rallying cry as good
>as kill him for his treachery,
>his lack of humility,
>his refusal to be whatever
>it is they think he should be.
>
>A mob has reasons
>that reason knows nothing of.
>Gathered together, it shouts,
>laughs,
>>cries,
>>>applauds;
>
>each person doing so because
>those in nearby seats are.
>The lights go down, and we glory
>in being part of something larger
>and the way a stone fits the hand.

Jupiter descends in thunder and lightning, sitting upon an eagle.

> His arrival is unexpected.
> There had been nothing
> to suggest any kind of divinity,
> then suddenly a God descends
> complete with theatrical effects
> and, oddly, specified transportation.
> (Other plays don't say,
> "Juliet Enters in Mini Cooper"
> or "Exit Hamlet. Sound of motorcycle.")
> So what the hell is this?
> We feel betrayed or, at least, confused.
> Is he serious? Mocking us? Lazy?
>
> But maybe this is the desired effect.
> A disbelief similar to wonder.
> What is more awe-inspiring,
> after all, than a God's appearance,
> unanticipated, unasked for,
> and undeniably in front of you?
>
> If we're honest, we'll admit
> a certain delight. We want to believe,
> and this seems, somehow, right.
> Everyone knows gods have a flair
> for the melodramatic, and they'll come
> when they feel like coming, regardless
> of what anyone wants or expects,
> then they'll insist on rerouting the story
> like cops directing traffic around
> seemingly impassable accidents.
> When they're done, they won't stay
> to take questions or suggestions,
> they'll just get back on their damn birds,
> and ride them, inscrutably, into the sky.

Hermione, like a statue

Sometimes we meet old friends
and wonder what has happened
to their faces

       …Botox?
             …a stroke?
                  … grief?

Have the years turned them to stone?
Or are they simply playing dead,
like possums, waiting for us to go?

And are they distressed by the changes
in us? By our faces and hands?
Or are they amazed how underneath
we seem the same as we once were,
having hardened into lives
that appear impressively life-like.

Enter Time, the Chorus

    Murders
                          Marriages
        Rapes
               Invasions
    Shipwrecks
                          Bed tricks
        Births
    Abandonments
                      Dismemberments,

they happen offstage,
                between scenes.

In that moment of darkness,
that brief rupture that can last
years,
        the world gets rearranged.

You had conversations with people
late into the night
                      slept with them
lived with them
        and they are
dead now,
        although you don't know it,
        or wounded
                      or wedded.

You travel on
        ignorant

of how coastlines and borders
have changed
        and are changing yet,
of how harbors you once sheltered in,
    long ago,
                silted shut.

Ferdinand and Miranda playing at chess

After he again professes his love and swears
he will always protect her, she tells him
about the time she played with her father
and she had insisted he had to let her win
because she was a kid. His face had clouded,
and he had replied by taking her pieces,
one by one. By the time he took her queen,
saving it for last, she was sobbing it wasn't fair.
He checkmated her, then made her play again.
Then again. So, she says to Ferdinand, who listens,
afraid to move, I learned early on how the game
is played, and how quickly a storm can arrive.
Make all the forecasts you like. Even on an island
this small, we live with unpredictable weather.

Exit, pursued by a bear

i.
The early drafts show
it wasn't an obvious choice.
Exit pursued by a wolf.
Exit pursued by a boar,
He had intended to rent
whatever animal they needed
then he heard the Beargarden
was clearing out damaged stock,
so he walked over with Burbage.
Most were too far gone
to be anything but meat,
but there was one,
too small and slow to be baited,
but impressive enough for a stage.
A chance to get an effect cheap,
that's what he told himself,
but sensed there was more to it
as he looked at the bear
and the bear looked him.

ii.
He recognizes it's a sweet gig.
Instead of being pitted against dogs,
wolves, or bulls, he just lumbers
across the stage in pursuit of an actor.
Thirty seconds a night, then he's done,
and the reaction is always gratifying.
God's Teeth! It's a bear! A real bear!
The wonder at nature unleashed
right there on the stage. The thrill
that he seems tame, but who knows
what he'll do or where he'll go.

But, although he appreciates the role,
he knows he's no Sackerson

and it's not a play with legs,
so he worries about what will happen
at the end of the run. At best,
he'll be unloaded to a traveling troupe,
but it's more likely he'll end up
a rug, a coat, steaks on a pub menu.
Thinking about this makes him
a little more ferocious each night,
and he fantasizes about
a final performance where
there is no exit, just "pursued by,"
the same ending, only bloodier.

iii.
Instead of getting used to the scene,
each time it takes the actor longer
to calm down once he reaches the wings.
Yes, the bear's old, slow, and usually drunk,
but still it's a bear, one who seems pissed,
and who has teeth and claws, and
who gets closer and closer.

iv.
She's seen every performance, and
each time she hopes Antigonus will be okay,
that, like Hermione and the baby,
somehow he will survive,
that it will end up being a mistake,
and the grief of his wife will be redeemed,
but no, he always dies, getting hunted down
and pulled apart as he calls for help.
No matter what story we expect
or want, this is how it goes.
You can run. You can submit
to the chemo and operations.
You can sidle to one side, hoping

to place yourself out of the way.
Sometimes you can even become
so involved in the action
you forget the bear is there,
but it is. Always. Snuffling
in the wings. Outside the theater.
In the bloodstream. Closing in.

v.

Heminges was surprised
to see the tied-up animal pawing
at nutshells in the pit of the Globe.
"You know," he pointed out,
"We don't need a real bear.
Just give someone a mask,
or use a puppet, or a sheet,
or have the actor say, 'Sblood!
Is that a bear behind me?'"
When the playwright didn't respond,
the theater manager continued,
"It's going to shit on stage,
and then where's your tragedy?"
Burbage interjected, "I thought
it was going to be a comedy."
Still Shakespeare said nothing,
and finally his friends recognized
that blank expression, that animal gaze.
He had left them. Once again
he was pursuing something
in his mind's eye. Or being pursued.

Enter King Henry

> "... The King's players had a new play, called *All is True*, representing some principal pieces of the reign of Henry VIII, which was set forth with many extraordinary circumstances of pomp and majesty ... sufficient in truth within a while to make greatness very familiar, if not ridiculous. Now, King Henry making a masque at the Cardinal Wolsey's house, and certain chambers being shot off at his entry, some of the paper, or other stuff, wherewith one of them was stopped, did light on the thatch, where being thought at first but an idle smoke, and their eyes more attentive to the show, it kindled inwardly, and ran round like a train, consuming within less than an hour the whole house to the very grounds."
>
> —Sir Henry Wotton, witness to the burning down of the Globe during a performance of *Henry VIII*

Having told him to make no public statement
about any aspect of the case until it was settled,
his lawyers were annoyed at the video footage
that surfaced on the internet. It had been taken
at some Spotlight on Playwrights! roundtable
by someone who clearly had been more interested
in Beaumont and Fletcher, zooming in each time
one of them spoke, but since he was between them
his comments had been recorded as well.
He had offered a few amusing anecdotes
about Marlowe, Will Kemp, and Queen Elizabeth,
but for the most part he had let the other panelists
hold forth, something Jonson was happy to do.
Towards the end, a young drama student had stood
and said, "Will, I just want to thank you so much
for coming and sharing. My mother loves your work,
and I was wondering if you have any advice
for people like me who are just starting out,
or maybe, you know, any overall thoughts
about your career or about ... you know ... all of it...."
He had arched an eyebrow, repeated "All of it?"
making the audience laugh. "My last play with John
was titled, 'All Is True.' Maybe that should be

my final comment, but …" he had paused to think,
or at least to give the impression of thinking
and then he had said, "Using a real bear?
That was a good idea. That worked.
A real cannon? That was a bad idea."

Exit

He writes the last stage direction,
then disappears from the London scene
returning to Stratford-on-Avon
where he tends the lawn, hangs out at Panera,
argues with his wife about bedroom furniture.
Occasionally people point him out
as a guy who used to be a player,

or they'll notice the plate—"Bard #1"—
but he'll pretend not to see them
as he drinks decaf with the other retirees,
the ones who have managed to survive,
and they kvetch about the government,
how things aren't what they were,
the sorry state of the globe.

Sources for Stage Directions

Enter the Duchess in a white sheet – *King Henry VI, Part II*
Exit at another door with the body of his son – *Henry VI, Part III*
Exit at one door with the body of his father – *Henry VI, Part III*
Exit with the body – *Henry VI, Part III*
Dead March – *King Henry VI, Part I*
Enter a Messenger with two heads and a hand – *Titus Andronicus*
She picks up some pieces – *Two Gentlemen of Verona*
Enter Kate – *The Taming of the Shrew*
Enter Hortensio with his head broke – *The Taming of the Shrew*
Enter aloft the drunkard… – *The Taming of the Shrew*
Enter the Queen with her hair about her ears – *Richard III*
Enter Richard and Buckingham in rotten armor, marvelous ill-favored – *Richard III*
The clock striketh – *Richard III*
Exeunt omnes, as fast as may be, frightened – *Comedy of Errors*
Enter Armado – *Love's Labour's Lost*
Enter Romeo and Juliet, above, at the window – *Romeo and Juliet*
Enter Friar John – *Romeo and Juliet*
Enter at the other end of the churchyard, Friar Laurence, with a lantern, crow, and spade – *Romeo and Juliet*
Enter Romeo. Enter Juliet – *Romeo and Juliet*
Enter Bottom – *Midsummer Night's Dream*
Exit, the Bastard – *King John*
Enter Gardeners – *Richard II*
Enter the travellers – *King Henry IV, Part I*
Falstaff Riseth Up – *King Henry IV, Part I*
Enter Prince of Wales… – *King Henry IV, Part I*
Enter Falstaff wearing a buck's head – *The Merry Wives of Windsor*
Enter Rumor, Painted Full of Tongues – *King Henry IV, Part II*
Enter the King in his nightgown, alone – *King Henry IV, Part II*
Enter Shylock – *The Merchant of Venus*
Exeunt Portia and Nerissa – *The Merchant of Venus*
Enter Benedick, alone – *Much Ado About Nothing*
Enter Innogen – *Much Ado About Nothing*
Enter Ambassadors of France – *King Henry V*
Enter Cinna, the Poet – *Jules Caesar*
Enter *Jacques*, and *Lords* ([like]) *Foresters*) [with a dead deer] – *As You Like It*

Enter Ghost – *Hamlet* and *Macbeth* and . . .
Flourish. Exeunt all but Hamlet – *Hamlet*
Enter Gertrude – *Hamlet*
Enter Ophelia – *Hamlet*
Enter Hamlet   – *Hamlet*
Enter Polonius – *Hamlet*
Enter Horatio – *Hamlet*
Enter Othello and Desdemona in Her Bed – *Othello*
Enter Viola, a Captain, and Sailors – *Twelfth Night*
Enter Cassandra Raving – *Troilus and Cressida*
Enter Helena – *All's Well That Ends Well*
Enter Poet, Painter, Jeweler, Merchant, and Mercer, at several doors – *Timon of Athens*
Enter Steward, with many bills in his hand – *Timon of Athens*
Enter Duke [disguised] – *Measure for Measure*
Enter Lucio and two other gentlemen – *Measure for Measure*
Exit Running. Attendants Follow – *King Lear*
Enter Lady Macbeth – *Macbeth*
Enter Lady Macbeth Reading a Letter – *Macbeth*
Thunder and Lightning. Enter Three Witches – *Macbeth*
Oboes and Torches – *Macbeth*
Enter Pericles, wet – *Pericles*
Enter a company of mutinous Citizens, with staves, clubs, and other weapons – *Coriolanus*
Jupiter descends in thunder and lightning, sitting upon an eagle – *Cymbeline*
Hermione, Like a Statue – *The Winter's Tale*
Enter Time, the Chorus – *The Winter's Tale*
Ferdinand and Miranda playing at chess – *The Tempest*
Exit, Pursued By a Bear – *The Winter's Tale*
Enter King Henry – *Henry VIII*

A professor at the University of North Carolina School of the Arts, JOSEPH MILLS holds an endowed chair, the Susan Burress Wall Distinguished Professorship in the Humanities. He has published sixth collections of poetry with Press 53. His book *This Miraculous Turning* was awarded the 2015 Roanoke-Chowan Award for Poetry, and his collection *Angels, Thieves, and Winemakers* was called "a must have for wine lovers" by the *Washington Post*. His poetry has been featured several times on Garrison Keillor's *The Writer's Almanac* and in former United States Poet Laureate Ted Kooser's nationally syndicated newspaper column, "American Life in Poetry." In addition to his volumes of poetry, he has researched and written two editions of *A Guide to North Carolina's Wineries* with his wife, Danielle Tarmey. He also has edited a collection of film criticism *A Century of the Marx Brothers*. He has degrees in literature from the University of Chicago, the University of New Mexico, and the University of California, Davis. More information about his work is available at www.josephrobertmills.com

www.ingramcontent.com/pod-product-compliance
Lightning Source LLC
LaVergne TN
LVHW041343080426
835512LV00006B/601